The African Presence in Santo Domingo

T0158412

Ruth Simms Hamilton
AFRICAN DIASPORA SERIES

THE AFRICAN PRESENCE IN SANTO DOMINGO

CARLOS ANDÚJAR

Translated by ROSA MARIA ANDÚJAR

MICHIGAN STATE UNIVERSITY PRESS · *East Lansing*

♾ The paper used in this publication meets the minimum requirements
of ANSI/NISO Z39.48-1992 (R 1997) (Permanence of Paper).

Michigan State University Press
East Lansing, Michigan 48823-5245

Printed and bound in the United States of America.

18   17   16   15   14   13   12   1   2   3   4   5   6   7   8   9   10

LIBRARY OF CONGRESS CATALOGING-IN-PUBLICATION DATA
Andújar Persinal, Carlos, 1956–
[Presencia negra en Santo Domingo. English]
The African presence in Santo Domingo / Carlos Andújar ; translated by Rosa Maria Andújar.
p. cm. — (Ruth Simms Hamilton African Diaspora series)
Includes bibliographical references.
ISBN 978-1-61186-042-9 (pbk. : alk. paper) 1. Blacks—Dominican Republic—History. 2. Slavery—Dominican
Republic—History. 3. Dominican Republic—Civilization—African influences. I. Title.
F1941.B55A6313 2012
972.93'00496—dc23
2011036830

Book design by Charlie Sharp, Sharp Des!gns, Lansing, Michigan
Cover design by Erin Kirk New
Cover photo: A woman practicing the African tradition of carrying a load on the head.

Michigan State University Press is a member of the Green Press Initiative and is committed
to developing and encouraging ecologically responsible publishing practices. For more
information about the Green Press Initiative and the use of recycled paper in book
publishing, please visit www.greenpressinitiative.org.

Visit Michigan State University Press at www.msupress.org

Contents

SERIES EDITOR'S FOREWORD, *Kimberly Eison Simmons* vii

FOREWORD, *C. E. Deive* xi

PREFACE xv

Introduction. 3

West Africa during the Fifteenth and Sixteenth Centuries 7

The Slave Trade 15

The Origins of Slaves 19

Slavery in Santo Domingo 29

Black Rebellions 37

Contributions of Black Culture to Dominican Culture 51

Conclusions 61

NOTES 63

BIBLIOGRAPHY 69

Series Editor's Foreword

Kimberly Eison Simmons

A
s book series editor, I am pleased to have this book in the Ruth
Simms Hamilton African Diaspora Research Project Book Series.
Carlos Andújar is known throughout the Dominican Republic as
a scholar of Afro-Dominican history, culture, and identity. I first became
aware of his work, and other Dominican scholars working on similar issues,
when I was a graduate student at Michigan State University (1994–2000). I
was in the doctoral program in Anthropology, and I was also a Researcher-
in-Residence with the African Diaspora Research Project (ADRP) under the
direction of the late Ruth Simms Hamilton, who was a mentor, professor,
and friend. This book series is named in her honor—paying tribute to her
and her pioneering work in African Diaspora Studies.

As students, Dr. Hamilton encouraged us to embrace and interact
with the African Diaspora in our academic lives. Many of us read literature in different languages and included the voices of scholars outside
of the United States in our work. In fact, many students in the ADRP

represented African diasporic communities outside the United States; from Brazil, to Puerto Rico, Panama, the Dominican Republic, and Kenya, they brought their experiences with them. In addition to ADRP seminars, Dr. Hamilton organized conferences and published a monograph based on the proceedings (1990) as well as *Conexões*, the ADRP newsletter. These efforts were far-reaching—the attempt was to make sure that people of African descent were connected, engaged, and subjects of their history, not just objects of study.

Given Dr. Hamilton's inclusive approach, I am certain that she would have encouraged book series submissions from scholars throughout the Diaspora. For this reason in particular, I am pleased to include Carlos Andújar's *La presencia negra en Santo Domingo* (*The African Presence in Santo Domingo*) as the first translated book in the series. Originally published in 1997, *La presencia negra* is a seminal work of Afro-Dominican history and experience. We were fortunate to have Rosa Maria Andújar, Carlos's sister, translate the Spanish text to English. Having the book available in English gives scholars outside of the Dominican Republic an opportunity to learn about the social and cultural issues presented and discussed from the "inside," and in this case, by a Dominican scholar. In other words, it broadens the discussion.

In the book, Andújar argues that Dominican elites made concerted efforts to conceal the African past over time. Through a discussion of West African influences, he discusses the African contributions to Dominican society and culture—from food to linguistics and music:

> Foremost in importance is the contribution of black slaves to Domini-
> can magic-religion, as well as to the music, diet, language, economy,
> social organization, customs, ornaments, and body language,

bequeathed not only by Africans, but also by slaves of other Caribbean islands who later immigrated to the country as farm workers.

He continues the discussion by exploring other cultural practices and traditions with connections to Africa, and claims them as part of the Dominican collective:

Each of our gestures, our food, colors, dances, music—as well as some religious expressions, turns of phrase, names of places, burial rites, crafts, and other objects—bear witness to that past. Evidence of that is the presence/persistence of blackness in those things in which people routinely partake: food, gestures, form and color of dress, dance and music, religious beliefs, turns of phrase, place names, funeral rites, artisanship, and objects that represent culture in a material way.

Going against the grain, rather than exploring issues of *Hispanidad* (an appreciation for everything Spanish) or contributions of the Taínos to Dominican society, Andújar opts to map connections to Africa and shows that there is an African presence in Santo Domingo, from the past to the present, and this is made evident by considering contemporary cultural practices and production in the Dominican Republic.

Foreword

C. E. Deive

C arlos Andújar is an enthusiastic, determined scholar of African American society. Very few social scholars in Santo Domingo have seriously dared to address, without prejudice, such a controversial and yet exciting subject as the one regarding the contribution of black slaves to Dominican culture.

Until 1973, the year of the First Symposium on African Presence in the Antilles, held at the Universidad Autónoma de Santo Domingo, it was a common belief that the Dominican Republic was a nation of pure Hispanic cultural characteristics—free, therefore, of any links to Africa or Haiti.

Language, religion, family organization, and customs—key components, among others, of every culture—were claimed to be bequeathed exclusively by Spain and to have remained intact, with no additional influences on our ethos. The Hispanic, we were told, was civilized and pure, while that which was Haitian and African had to be rejected as spurious and wild.

Surmounting the obstacles imposed by the Trujillo ideology,[1] which made Caucasians of Dominicans and "white creoles" of blacks, a small group of historians, sociologists, and anthropologists started to fight the myth that for years identified us as culturally Spanish, and most importantly, to reveal what had been obvious throughout our history: the existence of clearly African traits and behavior patterns in Dominican culture.

This work summarizes, with a truly enviable economy of means, the results of a variety of research in Afro-Dominican studies. This is, by all means, the intention of the author, as noted in the introduction.

This detailed work, which synthesizes with remarkable efficacy the achievements attained so far in the analysis and understanding of the black presence in the Dominican culture, covers a far more important subject than many would like to acknowledge. So important and essential, indeed, that without it our history and sociocultural life could not be understood.

The author begins with a summary of West African cultures during the fifteenth and sixteenth centuries—that is, the era of exploration of that continent and the slave trade to Europe and America—followed by a brief discussion about the slave trade itself, the tribal origins of slaves brought to Santo Domingo, the characteristics of slave production in the colony, and the slave rebellions that emerged as an inevitable consequence.

This section helps to create a better understanding of the very forms and processes that gave the Dominican Republic the African features that it shares with other countries of the region, and also its particularities in many respects.

Foremost in importance is the contribution of black slaves to Dominican magic-religion, as well as to the music, diet, language, economy, social organization, customs, ornaments, and body language—bequeathed not only by Africans, but also by slaves of other Caribbean islands who later immigrated to the country as farm workers.

Carlos Andújar not only exposes the minimal research done by other authors. As a sociologist concerned with Dominican history, its origins and characteristics, he follows an analysis of what he calls "the Dominican case" with regard to the blacks in our culture, with all the prejudices and false values leading to the concealment and misrepresentation of that presence.

Particularly interesting are the observations about the people's misperception of their own ethnic and cultural identity—a misperception cultivated by the ruling class in defense of their economic interests.

In every way enhancing Dominican literature, easy and enjoyable to read, *The African Presence in Santo Domingo* is an essay written with strict adherence to the truth and using the most appropriate theoretical and methodological tools, allowing us to enter the fascinating world of that other face of Dominican history that doctrinaire Hispanophiles have tried to steal from us.

Preface

The ethnohistorical approach of this work came to me in 1991 as I participated in an international seminar held in San Juan, Puerto Rico, on "Ancestor Worship in the Caribbean," organized by the University of Puerto Rico.

This work is the result of my encounter, in San Juan, with Mexican researcher Luz Martinez Montiel, and a *babalao* (priest) of the Yoruba religion and Cuban researcher, resident in Puerto Rico, Chiqui-Irminio Valdez (now deceased). Our conversations led to this ethnohistorical approach, whose material would be published in the proceedings of a conference called "The Third Root" in Mexico in 1992.

After thinking about it, I agreed to commit to my colleagues and a new challenge. I was not asked for more than I could give on this book. On the other hand I foresaw the importance of such a work, which would synthesize all that had been said on the matter.

Among an array of difficulties, I undertook the job and, when completed, sent it to Mexico in 1992. Unfortunately, for financial reasons, the confer-ence could not be carried out on that occasion. Indeed, an international seminar with the same name was programmed for that same year and would address the input of different black groups into American societies.

I then decided to work on making some corrections to the original ver-sion, with prior authorization of those responsible for the conference in Mexico; I continued up until its publication in Santo Domingo, where it will undoubtedly fulfill its commitment.

I was also prompted to publish this because, as a university professor, I was so aware of the lack of material in this field for those studying our history and culture.

Leaving behind all the circumstances surrounding this work, I offer it to the public, with the hope that it will contribute to the discussion of some aspects regarding the black community in our country.

The writing is organized in short chapters, allowing a reflection on each particular case, while keeping the chronological sequence.

THE AFRICAN PRESENCE
IN SANTO DOMINGO

Introduction

Research on the role played by African civilizations in the shaping of Latin American societies is rare. Several reasons explain this lack of information. Widespread prejudices and distortions have prevailed in intellectual reflections about the region, both stemming from the influence exerted by the "Establishment" and its efforts to remove any black culture element of expression from American societies.

Despite such concealment, the influence of black slaves of the late sixteenth century on the ethnic identity of the region is indisputable. In mainstream explanations of our cultural legacy, the dominant groups of our society have privileged Hispanic or European values. In the Caribbean, for instance, references to the sociocultural role played by pre-Columbian peoples are evasive, and nuanced with romantic metaphors.

Mexico is an exception where, although somewhat ambivalent, an awareness regarding the importance of the Aztec culture has taken its place in the mind and life of Mexican people.[2] In other countries and regions of

Latin America, we are still in a debate about cultural "being" and "nonbe-ing"—that is, between *being real* (culturally speaking) or being a *cultural fiction*.[3] In the Caribbean, this dichotomy is historically enhanced by the ethnocide of the aboriginal population, which implies the absence of their culture as part of regional identity.

Hence, in the Caribbean culture, being black is still a taboo subject. In the Dominican Republic, theoretical reflections on the matter began only two decades ago at a conference held at the Universidad Autónoma de Santo Domingo.[4] Previous works were unsystematic and imbued with the Hispanic prejudices that permeated the thinking of most authors. This, however, does not undermine their relevance.

In the Dominican Republic, prejudice is outweighed by the mixing of the population, which not only complicates any serious research on the subject, but—coupled with the racist tradition described above—creates a somewhat demeaning climate for any discussion related to the black community.[5] Dominicans reject their black roots, as might be expected in a population of highly mixed blood individuals, producing a picture of bleak alienation.[6]

This distortion has created a conscious and subconscious racism, resulting in the avoidance of everything implying and identifiable as black roots.[7] But since, according to Clyde Kluckhohn, "culture has an irrational layer [sub-conscious, we would add], in their daily life Dominicans express much of their black heritage, for instance their eating habits, their body language . . . as noticed by Peruvian folklorist and poet Nicomedes Santa Cruz."[8]

This issue is addressed with the intention of challenging the existing marginalization, because today, although more flexible, as the object of academic study the subject is still limited to a small group of researchers.

In our opinion, in the Dominican Republic there is no real concern about this forbidden truth of our history and our current lives. The issue remains undervalued, or in any case concerns only a small group of scholars. It is important, though, to point out that we do not endorse the partiality of some African studies, prone to exaggeration, to forms of racism or theoretical simplicity, and endowing Africa with a preponderant influence in the development of our cultural ethos. This type of attitude would lead us to the same mistakes made in the theoretical, philosophical, and methodological views of pro-Hispanic visions.

Caribbean cultures are a perfect hybrid, where it is difficult to separate the traits of African and European heritage. Culture cannot isolate its patterns as we isolate water and oil. In proceedings arising from the "cultural fact,"[9] theoretical models cannot be detached from their own analysis, since these processes are not only temporary, but are influenced by pressures, encounters, loans, etc. This structure is what we call "real culture."[10]

Our people have lived ignoring each other; this is a fact, at least in the Dominican Republic and in its interrelation with the rest of the Caribbean. For these reasons, it is our aim to fulfill a role in the discussion of culture, on the understanding that every effort should be directed towards finding ourselves and, from that perspective, rethinking the future. It is also our goal to contribute to the effort to put in its proper dimensions the input of the African peoples who came to the Americas, and who today, scattered across the hemisphere, not only give color, joy, and rhythm, together with other Latin American peoples in the amalgam, but also add meaning to life, and prospects for a better tomorrow.

West Africa during the Fifteenth and Sixteenth Centuries

For many people, including social scientists, the degree of development of African peoples at the moment of the encounter between Africa and the Americas is surprising. The similarities in behavior make one consider the first the ancestor of the second, but especially the ancestor of the Caribbean. Two major factors at this point are crucial in history: (1) the "discovery" of the continent by Christopher Columbus and the subsequent process of colonization and slavery, and (2) the initiation and development of the slave trade in the fifteenth century.

The splendor and contributions to society characteristic of sub-Saharan or negroid African cultures are barely known. The illiteracy of most of them, among other elements, was long considered by traditional historians as a constraint for study. There is almost no knowledge, for instance, about the magnificence of black African peoples. Consider the large empires, kingdoms, and states, as well as the rise of science, commerce, arts, urbanization, strong military and economic power, that stand out in the study of the Mali Empire, for instance. In order to overcome these false beliefs, our impressions of Africa need to be rethought, as does the belief that Africa's material backwardness is due to biological "backwardness." Fortunately, sponsored by UNESCO, eight volumes are being written on the general history of Africa, which will help unfold the truth about Africa and its magnificent past.

By the time of the arrival of Europeans to the African continent, major civilizations had already been developed. Blacks who came to the Americas—according to Herskovits—came primarily from the west coast and surrounding areas (an average of 200 kilometers inland), and shared a similar social development, that is, the same cultural patterns. However, black slaves came from different places, and their religious practices varied from black animism to polytheism and Islam.[11]

Similar differentiation occurs when studying the characteristics of the social structures of these peoples. First in line would be those from tribal societies, organized under the rules of descent, like some located on the western coasts, as opposed to those coming from centralized states, many of which became kingdoms or empires, such as the strip of Sudan.

This outstanding development is, for many authors, linked to the expansion of Islam in black Africa, which began in the twelfth century, and whose philosophical-religious platform was open to "Africanization," as some call the process of accommodation and flexibility of Islam to the African culture. The main impact, however, of Islam on sub-Saharan cultures was the development of the market and its opposition to black slavery. Although trade routes through the Sahara had existed long before, the spread of Islam in Africa increased their magnitude, driving major cities to become real centers of commerce, such as Gao, Kano, Timbuktu, and others.

The Kingdoms of the Sudan

The Mali Empire

Among the kingdoms of the southern strip of the Sahara, Mali was by far the most important. After its foundation in 1235 and the reunification of the three main provinces, Do, Kiri, and Bako, under the aegis of King Sunjata Keyta—who immediately became *mansa* (emperor)—began what is known as the first *mandinga* or *mandé* expansion.[12]

Besides archaeology and oral tradition, sources for studying the history of the Mali Empire come from the documents of the scribe Al-Bakri, and later of the geographer Al-Idvrisi.

Known for its abundance of gold, its main resources and economic power came from agriculture and livestock. This boom led not only to a large population, but also to villages that reflected the economic growth of the empire. Some sources estimate the population at 40 to 50 million inhabitants.[13]

Two events highlighted the wealth of the empire, both linked to one of its most eccentric rulers, Mansa Musa I (1307 to 1332), who professed the Islamic religion: (1) his pilgrimage to Mecca; and (2) his claims about possibly having visited the land later known as America, which nobody had ever heard about. Whatever the truth is, his immense power is undeniable. Mansa Musa I is alleged to have said during his trip to Cairo, speaking about the sovereign Sunjaba II, who ruled before him: "He did not understand that it was impossible to reach the end of the surrounding sea; he attempted it and perished in the attempt."[14]

According to Jeffer and Weiner, the *malinkes*[15] were in America (in the "outer surrounding waters," that is, the Atlantic) about two hundred years before Christopher Columbus.[16] However, no proof of the assertion of Mansa Musa I has ever been found.

As for his trip to Mecca, we read: "Mansa Musa had a large entourage, carrying with him 80 packets of powdered gold, 3,800 kgs each, accompanied by 60,000 porters and preceded by 500 slaves, each carrying a stick weighing 3 kgs."[17]

After 1375, cartographers began depicting Mansa Musa's image on maps of Sudan, holding in his hand a gold nugget, a symbol of wealth acknowledged even outside the Sudanese territory. Other empires did not reach this level of opulence.

The Songhay Empire

Founded towards the end of the fifteenth century with its capital in Gao, Songhay had already begun to take shape as an empire in the eleventh century, according to oral tradition and documents written by Adsa'dí and A. Kati.

Its economy was based on fishing, livestock, agriculture, and trans-Saharan commerce. The economy would be developed in the direction of North Africa and later towards the Mediterranean, mainly by the sale of gold, slaves, spices, ivory, and kola nuts.

Timbuktu, considered the holy city of Sudan, was conquered by the Songhay by 1468, reaching its apogee in the sixteenth century. At the time, the estimated population was about 80,000 inhabitants.

Timbuktu not only flourished because of its location along the trans-Saharan route, but also became a city of science and knowledge. It was the site of one of the largest black African universities. Professors from Cairo and other cities taught Islamic theology, law, grammar, rhetoric, astronomy, history, etc.

The empire's major cities each had their own differentiating features with regard to the others. The estimated population of Gao at the time was 100,000 inhabitants, which reflects its importance as an urban center.

The Kanem Empire

This vast empire was developed in the region of Chad, around the twelfth century. The *diwan* (writings produced by the chroniclers of the court) and oral tradition may help reconstruct part of its past. Apparently, the power and raison d'être of the empire were linked to the existence of its trans-Saharan market—primarily the slave trade, although its wealth was based on farming, ranching, and mining (mainly salt). In this context, the slave was regarded as the principal instrument of barter. After the sixteenth century, because of war in Europe, the rule of the empire was weakened and its importance decreased.

The Kingdom of Hawsa

With Kano as its main city, the kingdom of Hawsa is of uncertain provenance.[18] According to some authors, the population of the region occurred as a result of immigration from the declining Mali and Songhay empires.

Agriculture was the most important activity, fostered by fertile and productive land. The basic produce was wheat, rice, sorghum, and cotton for export. In its socioeconomic structure, artisans and merchants used cotton, salt, and slaves as their currency in regional exchanges.

Coastal Region (Guinea, Benin, and Yoruba)

In the coastal states, we can see a greater fragmentation of political and social organization, structured according to lineage. Although they traded other products, their economies were originally associated with the trade of kola nuts with the peoples of the Sudanese savannah and forests.

Agriculture was their main activity—especially rice cultivation in the lowlands and coastal wetlands—although to a lesser extent, some of these states were engaged in the extraction of salt, ivory, and slave trafficking. Only when the Europeans made contact with the region did the capture and sale of slaves become the main activity of most coastal towns, generating slave states such as Ashanti. Thus, the west coasts would soon become the point of attraction for business, replacing the northern region in this role.

In some parts, especially in Upper Volta-Cameroon, ironwork was known at an early stage, especially among the Yorubas, one of the major ethnic groups. In others, such as the towns of Oyo, Benin, and Ife, some more or less centralized states started to develop.

In towns such as Ife, sculptural art became popular, and statuettes were produced in clay, bronze, and wood. Of unique artistic value, bronze works from the Nupe kingdom came to influence the visual arts in Europe, placing Africa in a privileged place in the history of mankind despite its absence in "world history."

THE KINGDOMS OF CENTRAL AFRICA

The Kongo Empire

Known for its contact with the Portuguese in 1482, and discovered by Diego Cão, the kingdom of Bakongo is considered the largest in the south Sahara, covering several states. Its founders came from the ancient civilization of Luba. It is believed to have been founded between the late fourteenth century and the beginning of the fifteenth. Its capital was Mbanzakongo, and its king was known as *Manikongo* (Lord of the Kongo).

These people were considered excellent ironworkers, as well as skilled hunters and warriors. They developed pottery, weaving, and salt extraction, and used these as currency, like the little copper crosses and other coins called *nzimbu*. They developed the production of sea salt and the growing of crops such as bananas, yams, sugar cane, and peanuts.

Because of the extent of the territory, political control was exercised through local chiefs appointed by the king (*Manikongo*), accompanied by a council of elders. With time, however, these areas would slowly become small states with some autonomy. The most significant of these were the kingdoms of Ngoy, Kikongo, and Loango. There were others, less important, such as the region of Kwango Ndongo. In the area of Ndongo there was a hereditary title that later gave the name to the Portuguese colony of Angola, the *Ngola*.

By the seventeenth century, the region had more than two million people. In the early years, the Portuguese had excellent relations with the society that hosted them—to such an extent that most of the rulers of the kingdom of Kongo converted to Christianity. The *Manikongo* Nzinga Nkouvou converted to Christianity in 1491 (it is important, however, to clarify that many of these conversions were purely formal). In many cases, they changed their names for baptism, as was the case of *Manikongo* Alfonso I, who undertook a work of spreading Christianity so great that the capital of his kingdom was called the "city of church bells" (*ekongo dia ngungo*), and one of his sons was consecrated as a bishop in Rome in 1521.

Soon these relations were broken off because the Portuguese decided to begin the business of the slave trade. In 1575, Paulo Dias de Novias was sent to the countries of central Africa, this time as conqueror, changing the previous relationships with the region completely, especially the Kongo, which ended up declaring war with Portugal in 1650, and succumbing to the might of the European power.

The Slave Trade

By the year 1415, the Portuguese started exploring the African coast with the aim of finding a route to the East, pursuing spices, perfume, fabric, and gold from Sudan, the Far East, and Africa in general. Europe was highly appreciative of these goods. As Françoise Latour Da Veiga Pinto says: "The slave trade has gone hand in hand with the great Portuguese discoveries of the fifteenth century. . . . The economic motivations of the first sailors who came to Africa were of two kinds: to reach the sources of gold production of Sudan . . . and to discover a sea route to spices."[19]

The Portuguese began the slave trade business on August 8, 1414, when "for the first time there was a public sale of slaves in Lagos and in the presence of the Infante Don Enrique . . . . the best slaves were offered to the Church."[20] For his part, Fernando Ortiz states that, to facilitate this trade, in 1483 the Portuguese built a factory in San Jorge de Mina, selling blacks mainly from Benin, Gorée, Arguim, and Badagrí.[21]

For four centuries, Africa would supply slaves to the Americas for the establishment of plantation economies, and to Europe, as a benefit of the wealth produced overseas. The slave trade represented one of the bases of accumulation of capital, while African peoples were plunged into psycho-social depression by their ill fortune.

The basis of the trade was the exchange of goods between European (*Mongos*) and African slave traders. The first offered weapons, rum, and cloth, and the second, slaves. Three kingdoms stood out in this business: the Susus in the former French Guinea, the Vais of Sierra Leone, and the Ashantis in Ghana and Dahomey.

Although there were about two hundred slaves already in Hispaniola by 1501,[22] the real trade was formally started in 1517, with the landing in the West Indies of hundreds of black slaves from Spain and the western coasts of Africa.[23]

This influx of new labor would be the result of pressure from priests (*Jerónimos*)[24] and some neighbors of the colony, interested in developing large-scale sugar production.[25]

The trade is believed to have affected some 20 million blacks, 5 million of whom died due to the adverse conditions during the voyage.[26] Other authors give lower figures.

It is important to note, however, that at the time not only black Africans were slaves, but white prisoners and *moros*[27] were also subjected to the same conditions, sold for varying periods—including for life—along with their families, and destined for domestic labor. The treatment of these slaves did not differ substantially from that offered to blacks, and in some cases could be even worse. It is true that the first blacks who arrived in America were slaves, but this situation changed rapidly towards the second decade of the sixteenth century. As Frank Moya Pons stated: "Already in 1522 the business was booming; ships were coming from Seville to Santo Domingo and returned to the mainland with more than two thousand *arrobas* of sugar. Prices continued to rise, and with it the number of blacks consistently brought in to work in the mills. From now on, Indians and gold would be a lesser economic concern, while black destiny would be linked to the sugar industry until the end of that economy."[28] The view held by colonials in the West Indies was that "it is more profitable to buy them than to raise them"; this type of thinking led to an increased demand on the American coasts.

Fernando Ortiz mentions some of the goods received by the slavers in exchange for what was called "a *piece of the Indies.*"[29] For example, blacks should not have amputations, should be of good size and well built; in exchange the seller would receive large yellow amber, silver coins, red coral, knives, scarves, alcohol, iron bars, and guns.

This business was mainly observed off the coast of West Africa, because Europeans and especially the Portuguese could not penetrate inland without the risk of being killed by warrior groups, or by the effects of malaria, dengue, or yellow fever. Of those who did, very few returned to their ships, permanently moored off the beaches of Senegambia, Sierra Leone, and the Caleta of Benin—known as "white man's grave." This data made American anthropologist Melville Herskovits affirm that most of the slaves brought to America came from coastal tribes, of not more than 200 kilometers inland.[30]

The depletion of human resources made captors venture as far as the Upper Niger,[31] which would serve as a springboard in the traffic—like the cities of Kano and Gao, which fulfilled the role of host cities for the sale of slaves to Europeans.

It appears, thus, that a great number of blacks were from villages in which the *Twi, Yoruba,* and *Ewe* languages were spoken. Those villages belonged to what is Ghana, Benin, and Nigeria today. In the case of those captured by the Portuguese, the origins were Bantu groups settled in the area now occupied by Angola, Mozambique, and the Congo, and they were loaded at the port of San Jorge de Mina, in the Niger Delta.[32]

The control of the slave trade was taken from the Portuguese and Spanish by the English and the Dutch, who in 1672 formed the Royal African Company, which would regulate the trade until 1750, the year of its dissolution.

Legal provisions of King Carlos III, made around the same time, would affect the slave trade. By introducing economic and administrative changes, he eliminated the trade monopoly, which gave way to the legal concept known as "free trade." However, the Spanish American colonies needed the slave labor, and the metropolis could not be excluded from the smuggling of "pieces of the Indies." So the smuggling went on supplying the demand of the plantation economies of the Americas. Royal Charter 2827 states: "Every vessel of mine [said King Carlos III] in the vicinity of, or based in, Spain or the Indies can, on its own or on chartered boats, buy blacks wherever it can find the market, taking with it the money or goods that will be needed for the purchase. Introduction into these islands and provinces of Caracas will be free of all taxes."[33]

The importation of slaves continued, at least in Cuba, almost until the end of the nineteenth century. According to Ortiz, "On October 7, 1886, the patronage system was abolished and there were no more slaves in Cuba." With this measure, this degrading and ignominious economic system of racial exploitation came practically to an end.[34]

The Origins of Slaves

An exhaustive examination of what was Africa, as a continent and as a conjunction of cultures, will lead us way ahead of what is commonly believed or known. Africa had wealth, well-developed kingdoms and empires, reputed universities—a world as complex as that of Western countries. By so doing, we may gain a better understanding of those places that first provided labor to the Americas. It will also help to explain some persistent features in the culture of the Dominican Republic, despite the European influence.

In our search, some difficulties will, however, appear (errors in the transcription of ethnic names among others), which have been the subject of investigation for other scholars. These limitations are not only found in Santo Domingo but also in Cuba, Venezuela, and other places where the importation of blacks was not regulated. Additionally, when it came to slaves, importers would infringe the rules as much as possible in order to obtain a maximum of benefits at the lowest possible cost. In fact, shipping documents never existed. This is what Fernando Ortiz had to say on the subject: "Although a . . . law had ruled that only slaves coming from Angola, Guinea, the coast of Cape Verde, and neighboring islands could be brought to the Indies, greed was so great among slave merchants that the rules were not observed, and in Cuba, ethnologists could find all types of racial diversity in slaves from the intertropical regions that populated the west coast of Africa and, to a lesser extent, even slaves with east African origins."[35]

EAST AFRICA

Although the previous example refers to Cuba, the problem can be found in all regions in the Americas receiving black slaves. The slave trade had its beginnings in the villages of the far west coast (the region of Senegambia and Guinea), and then, through internal dynamics, it was moved down the Ivory Coast to the estuary of the Congo River at Angola.

Referring to the cultural zones and location of these groups, Carlos Larrazábal Blanco says: "Geographically, these cultures can be located, according to Aguirre Beltran cartograms: river tribes of Malagueta, the river tribes of Mina, the tribes of Carabalís, tribes of the Congo, and Angola tribes. In modern geography, these regions of the Atlantic Coast of Africa extend from the Senegal River to about the Cunene River . . . Gabon-Congo."[36]

The study of the African Diaspora must be approached from an anthropological perspective, thus allowing us a thorough view. Only in this way can we begin to clarify the existing level of confusion. Moreover, this perspective will allow us to handle data sources, achieving a balance that facilitates an accurate discernment and a logically correct approach.

Important aspects that hinder the study of the subject are:

- There are cases of two or more tribes with the same name.
- The slaves were designated according to the port of shipment or purchase: for example, blacks from the mines, coming from the Portuguese factory located at the estuary of the Congo River known as "San Jorge of Minas" or "Minas" Port.
- Smuggling was another reason for the misspelling of names.
- The changing of names also helped to disguise the origins of bellicose groups, which had less value in the market. Such is the case of *jelofes* and *yolofes*, known for their aggressive and warrior-like behavior.[37]

The list is not exhaustive. Adding to the confusion, there were also later changes to the names of places, cities, and ports to which were attributed vaguely European or even African origins. In some cases the names given at the moment of shipment or in the factory were those attributed by neighbors or adversaries.

Fernando Ortiz also highlights the sense of belonging of some slave groups who came from places of minor importance in Africa, but who, once they were in the Americas, referred to them as "great nations." The name change was not always accidental or arbitrary, as this author points out; names were also influenced by market expectations:

In the slave market it was important to specify the part of Africa you were buying from, because in spite of what some travelers and writers have said about the equality of all black Africans, buyers of slaves became accustomed to discovering important differences that would affect the price. The royal charter dated at Valladolid on June

6, 1556, provided the rate at which slaves should be sold in the West
Indies. If they came from São Tomé and Guinea, they should be sold
in Hispaniola, Cuba, and San Juan at 100 ducats per slave; those from
Cape Verde, 120 ducats.[38]

In Santo Domingo, the purchase of slaves reached its peak in the sixteenth century. In the perusal of parish books, official records, reports, bap-
tismal certificates, marriage certificates, death certificates, and inventories
of goods and properties (in which blacks were considered property), names
associated with Africa have been found. This documentation, however, is
not exhaustive.

In the Dominican Republic, two events affected the genealogical data
of the country: (1) the archives of the cathedral were burned almost entirely
during the invasion of the pirate Francis Drake, and (2) after Spain ceded
the western part of the island to France in the late eighteenth century, a
large number of documents belonging to the Royal High Court of Santo
Domingo became the possession of the island of Cuba.[39]

According to the lists compiled by C. E. Deive, during two periods of
our history (based on the study of names and their possible relationship
with places in Africa) Hispaniola had two sources that provided slaves.[40]
Between 1547 and 1606, twenty-eight ethnic groups were found (see
table 1).

TABLE 1. ETHNIC GROUPS IN HISPANIOLA BETWEEN 1547 AND 1606

Ambo	Angola	Barva	Bran
Anacasuanga	Arle	Biafara (Biafata)	Calabar (Carabí)
Anero	Banol (Banon)	Birsiri	Cazarga

Cosyna	Leme	Nanga	Vanín
Faula	Maga	Olofa (Olofe)	Viocho
Gambœ	Mandinga	Tenguerengue	Xolofo
Lacumí (Lucume)	Maricongo	Terranova	Zape

Most of these blacks came from Senegambia and Guinea, which by the sixteenth century were areas for the capture of slaves. However, between 1591 and 1821 this source changed, as can be seen in a compilation of names from the Congo and Angola region, whose origins were *Bantu* (see table 2).

TABLE 2. NAMES FOUND ASSOCIATED WITH AFRICA

Anará	Casanga	Mambo	Mondongo
Angola	Chamba (Chanvo)	Mandinga	Mutema
Ardá	Combel	Mango	Quisama
Bervisi	Congo	Manicongo	Sambu
Biafara	Fala	Matamba	Zabí
Bomba	Goimba	Mihi	Zape
Boumbi	Lucumí-Luango	Mingola	
Carabalí	Malemba	Mombo	

The repression that followed the 1796 uprising in Boca Nigua (close to the city of Santo Domingo) recorded the names of the imprisoned slaves and rebels: Francisco Sopó, Tomas Congo, José Mecu, Fermín Jara, Pedro Mondongo, etc. In all cases, we can see the names of ethnic groups acting as last names or designating the place of origin. These examples, among many others, permit the accurate reconstruction of the African ethnonym[41] in Santo Domingo.

TABLE 3. LIST OF AFRICAN TOPONYMY AND ETHNIC GROUPS

TOPONYMY	REGIONS OF AFRICAN ETHNIC GROUPS
Angola, Angola	Mbundu, Imbangala, Congo
Mina, Ghana, Togo	Ashanti
Lucumí, Nigeria	Yoruba
Loango, Congo	Bavili
Tari, Togo	Ewe
Arara, Dahomey (Benín)	Ewe, Fon
Gelofe, Senegal	Wolof
Malemba, Cabinda, Angola	Bayombe
Cabinda, Angola	Bayombe, Bavili, Congo
Carabalí, Nigeria	Efik, Ibibio
Congo, Congo	Congo
Matamba, Angola	Mbundu, Imbangala
Enbuyla, Congo	Congo
Nago, Nigeria	Yoruba

Other authors complete the list compiled by Deive.[42] To avoid repetition, and because sometimes the way in which authors write the name of ethnic groups varies, we have listed them in alphabetical order (see table 4).

TABLE 4. NAMES OF AFRICAN ORIGIN

Ambo	Andrá	Ashanti[†]	Bara[†]
Amboi*	Anero	Bamba	Barva
Ana[†]	Angola	Bambara	Baules
Anacasuanga	Arara	Banol	Bervisi

(TABLE 4 CONTINUED)

Bese	Cones*	Kpelle†	Menguí
Biafara-Biafata-	Congo-Kongo	Kukuruku†	Miga
Biaffara-Brafara	Cosyna	Leme	Miha-Mihi*
Bijoso	Cozin*	Limba†	Mina
Bodó*	Dan†	Locumi*	Mingola
Bolumbi	Diola†	Loko†	Molembo
Boruco	Espú	Longo*	Mondongo
Bran	Ewe†	Luango-Loanga†	Mongongo
Brison	Fala	Luarme*	Mono
Calabar	Fare	Lucume-Lucumi	Motemá
Calaun*	Faula	Lupolo†	Motembo*
Camba†	Fula†	Luqueme*	Munda
Can†	Gagu†	Maga	Mutema-Motema*
Cana	Gambu*	Makonde†	Ngombe†
Canga†	Gelofes†	Malemba	Ofori
Canguey	Goande†	Maleque†	Olofa
Carabalí	Guagua	Malinke	Olofe
Carabi	Guimbá	Mambo	Pamuest†
Casonga	Guimbú	Mandinga	Pana
Cazabí*	Guro†	Manga-Mongo*	Pende†
Cazarga	Jara	Manicongo	Popó†
Chamba†	Kagoro†	Matamba	Quima
Chonvo*	Kasonke†	Matundo-Matamba*	Quisama
Cita	Kisama†	Mbenbe	Saca
Cobele	Koko†	Mecoe	Sambu
Cobelo	Kono-Kona†	Melón*	Sania
Combelu*	Koranko†	Mende	Sena†

(TABLE 4 CONTINUED)

Senegui	Subolo	Vai[†]	Yara
Senegus	Tabí	Vanin	Yauru
Sengué	Tari[†]	Viocho	Yolofe-Gelofes[†]
Soliman[†]	Temne[†]	Wolof-Gelofes[†]	Yombe[†]
Soninke[†]	Tenguerengue	Xolofo	Yoruba[†]
Sopo-Supo[†]	Terranova	Yaguate*	Zape
Sose	Toma[†]	Yalunka[†]	Zaramo[†]

*C. Larrazábal Blanco, *Los Negros y la Esclavitud en Santo Domingo* (Santo Domingo: J. D. Postigo, 1975).
[†]F. Lizardo, *Cultura africana en Santo Domingo* (Santo Domingo: Sociedad Industrial Dominicana, 1979).

Referring to the obstacles to reconstruction based on available documents, and with regard to the efforts of both Larrazábal Blanco and Inchaustegui, Deive states: "The comparison of these two sources shows part of the difficulties outlined on the use of documents: the corruption in spelling many tribal names. Thus 'Minga' in Larrazábal Blanco becomes 'Maga' in Inchaustegui; 'Calum' (Larrazábal) and 'Calabar' (Inchaustegui); 'Cozin' (Larrazábal) and 'Cosyna' (Inchaustegui); 'Lucuma' (Inchaustegui)."

This suggests that the list contains names of previously repeated ethnic groups—not in the sense of its writing, but in the designated place. The confusion largely stimulates the efforts of specialists in clarifying matters. This would also contribute to the reconstruction of African history, as seen by Olabiyi B. Yai (see table 5).[43]

In the current state of the history of African peoples, the alignment of the transcriptions of names, places, and nations is part of the picture of the struggle for decolonization in which it plays a particular role.

TABLE 5. HOW AFRICAN NAMES WERE ASSIMILATED IN DIFFERENT LANGUAGES

ENGLISH	FRENCH	PORTUGUESE
Aja	Adja	Ajá
Hausa, Hawsa	Haoussa	Ussá, Auça, Hauça
Ashantee, Asante, Ashanti	Achanti, Ashanti	Axante, Achanti
Bambara, Banmana	Bámbara	Bámbara
Borno, Bornu	Bornou	Bornu
Jolof, Djolof	Jolot, Ouolof	Jolof, Yelofe
Damargu, Damergu	Damerghou⁰	—
Grusi	Gourounsi	Gurunxi, Grunce
Twi	Twi	Odji, Tshi
Songhai	Sonrhai, Songhay	—
Wagadu, Wagadugu	Ouagadougou	Uagadugu
Bamum	Pámom, Bamoum, Bamum	Pahouin
Manika	Manica, Manika	Manice
Monomotapa, MonoMwana	Monomotapa	Baracutuba
Mutapa, Mwene	Mutapa	—
Zimbabwe, Symbaoe	Zimbabwe, Zimbaboué	Zimbabue
Banguéla, Pangela	Benguela	Benguela
Arada	Allada, Arda, Ardres	Ardra
Fanta, Fanti, Fántee	Fanti, Fanté	Fante
Ketu	Kétou	Keto, Ketu, Queto
Ijesha, Ijesa	Jecha, Ijecha	Igexa, Gaxáa, Igesá
Benin, Bini	Bellin	Benin
Malkalanga	Karanga	Calanga
Zanzibar	Zanguebar, Zanzibar	—
Whydah	Ouidah, Whydah	Ajuda
Sosso, Susu	Soussou	Susu
Tapa, Nupe	Tara, Noupe	Nupe, Nifé, Nufa
Cabinda, Kabenda	Cabinda	Cabinda

SOURCE: O. B. Yai, *Ethnonymies et toponymies Africaines* (Paris: Unesco, 1984).

Accordingly, any proposal for such an alignment should come from a clear understanding of decolonization.

So far we can discern the complexity in the study of the Diaspora. Only an ethnohistorical approach offers the opportunity to perceive the reality of what happened, despite the limitations noted. It seems, however, obvious that the contingent of black slaves that settled in the Americas came mainly, at first, from the area of Guinea and Senegambia, and in later times from what is known as Congo-Angola—although it is possible to find, here or there, some names coming from other areas. This being so, it will define the ethnohistorical and cultural traits.

Slavery in Santo Domingo

Although the first blacks came to the island around 1496, a pattern of slavery was nonexistent at the time. However, we believe that moment began what would eventually, several decades later, become the classic form of exploitation implemented in the Americas by Europeans: the "sugar-cane plantation" economy.

This colonial plantation model had three types: cotton, coffee/cocoa, and sugar cane. Of these three, sugar cane was the one introduced in the Caribbean. Prior to sugar-cane plantations, Native Americans were used for the exploitation of gold. According to Tolentino Dipp: "After 1494, the exploitation of several different markets in Santo Domingo was considered a real failure. The aspirations of capitalist enterprises significantly changed; their dreams of gold and spices were dashed, and instead the easily available slave trade, although not a very large business as yet, inspired the babble of capitalist greed."[44]

In the Dominican Republic, and in the rest of Latin America, the sugar industry is inevitably linked to slavery. This explains why, when the gold economy was declining—among other reasons because of the discovery of Mexico and Peru, which provided large gold flows, and the drastic decline of the overutilized indigenous population—colonial groups linked to sugarcane interests felt the need to reorient the economy towards this market, for which they needed manpower.

A pioneer in this business was Hernando de Gorjón, who accumulated a considerable fortune during his eighteen years as *encomendero*. This is what Moya Pons has to say about it: "Like other wealthy men of Hispaniola, he had realized that gold would no longer be the major source of income as it had been in the past. So he decided to embark on the adventure of investing all his accumulated money . . . in the construction of mills to manufacture sugar and sell it to Europe."[45]

In Spain there were differences regarding sugar as a positive replacement for gold; therefore the planting of sugar cane, cassia (similar to cinnamon), and cotton was not initially appealing to the residents of La Vega and elsewhere in the Dominican Republic. Spain needed gold, not agricultural products. The agricultural contradictions found within a variety of plans for the economy caused, among other things, the "Rebellion of Roldán"—led by Francisco Roldán, heading those advocating for the distribution of Indians and for the development of gold exploitation. Analyzing the historical consequences of this fact, Juan Bosch states: "Roldán demanded and obtained land and Indians to work it, for him and his followers. He is considered the first *encomendero* in America, since his uprising led to the creation of the system at least four years before it was lawfully established."[46]

According to the Dominican priest Bartolomé de Las Casas, Pedro de Atienza, a resident of Concepcion de la Vega, was the first to plant sugar cane on the island in significant proportions. However, the chronicler Gonzalo Fernández de Oviedo y Valdés, commonly known as Oviedo, argues that the originator of the crop was Gonzalo de Velosa, along the Nigua River near the city of Santo Domingo, who was accompanied by experts coming from the Canary Islands, where the product had become popular. Sugar production, however, barely satisfied the local market.

This process culminated in the so-called "sugar economy," hosted not only by Las Casas, but by the colonial government of *los Jerónimos*.

The year 1517 marks the shift and, above all, the attitude change of the colony. "In the memorandums of Las Casas to the grand chancellor in 1517, in order to prevent the total destruction of Indians and to alleviate their condition . . . , Las Casas proposes that they be sent to [work] the crops along with some blacks. . . . [Also] the Spanish living in the islands be permitted the introduction of a number of blacks from Castilla."[47]

The initiatives taken by Las Casas, along with his statements in favor of replacing the indigenous with black labor, as well as his views on blacks, have generated an important debate about the humanity of this priest. For some historians, however, this idea of Las Casas's may be considered rather liberal when contrasted with the prevailing sociopolitical metropolitan context.

On August 18, 1518, the first license to import blacks was granted to the Baron de Montenay, Lorenzo Gramenot (known as Gouvenot/Gorrebot). By this means he was allowed to bring in 4,000 Christians or black *ladinos*,[48] considered more docile and manageable. Gramenot transferred the license to Genoese merchants. Slaves arrived a couple of years later.

The sugar industry reached its real apogee in 1522, when exports to Spain reached around 558,000 pounds. By that time, there were about forty sugar mills (some under construction) and several *trapiches* (generated by animal power), built with loans from the Spanish Crown. The impetus of this type of economy generated a great demand for labor and, subsequently, an increase in the plantation-related population. Tolentino Dipp estimates that by the end of the first quarter of the sixteenth century, the black population of Santo Domingo surpassed the white.[49]

Las Casas speaks of a population of 30,000 blacks to 60,000 whites, but the exact date of these figures is unknown. Other authors are decidedly more modest in their assessment and talk of a total population of 8,000 to 9,000 people, mostly blacks.[50]

Such a small population at the peak of the sugar industry reflects a limited economic development. An increased production rate would have shown a population growth more in accordance with the economy.

Furthermore, and especially around 1555, the colony experienced a paradoxical phenomenon: despite the slow collapse of the sugar industry, the establishments and licenses continued, in fact, throughout the whole century.

In a state of a semi-paralyzed economy, where their presence was superfluous, where were blacks going? Logically, we can guess that they were being smuggled to other islands of the Caribbean. Larrazábal Blanco outlines two reasons to support this inference: "Spain charged for each license and settlement of blacks. In 1556, Philip II increased the customs duties in the West Indies. . . . In 1572–1573 the king was compelled to sign a provision which obliged the authorities to charge for the rights of *almojarifazgo*[51] for all blacks introduced, just as for any other commodity."[52]

FACTORS IN THE SHARP DOWNTURN OF THE ECONOMY

Several assumptions could explain the rapid decline of the colonial sugar economy:

- The inability of local residents (settlers) to absorb the cost of the "pieces of the Indies." The financial situation of the settlers prevented them from purchasing slaves, and the Crown, although acknowledging the need for sugar production and that it was not available in the market, was not willing to help. Thus, this was the cause of early trouble with the slave labor that sustained the colonial sugar economy.

- Spain did not participate actively in the slave trade, but consented to it in exchange for a kind of tribute and/or taxes, thus leaving all risks to others. Spain would equally fail to invest in the purchase of slaves or ships or bartered goods, or in the crew.[53]

- The minimal participation of Spain in the slave business in the early decades of the sixteenth century would have a negative impact, because once in the Americas, blacks would be bought by the Spanish settlers, and they would have to pay tribute to the metropolis. That is, the Spanish monarchy did not seem too concerned with the development of the oligarchy or the sugar-plantation economy under its protectorate.[54]

- Another possible reason is related to the existence of another market. Spain banned the marketing of sugar in the European countries, particularly in Flanders, where there could have been a secure market. This depressed production on the island, in spite of the decision of the Crown to sell the sugar in Andalucía, which was an inappropriate marketing decision.

- An equally important factor is the impressive population boom in Mexico and Peru in the early years of the 1540s, and the resale of slaves in Puerto Rico and Cuba.

These combined factors led to the final collapse of the sugar industry around 1580. It was replaced by the only possible form of economy available to a society in conflict with this defined model: the *hatera* economy, based on land use and livestock. With little effort and investment, there was more than enough on the island. Due to its characteristics, raising livestock did not demand a large work force, and it was therefore an economy based on little effort.

The *hatera* economy made blacks a kind of serf: part of their time was allotted to working the land for the benefit of the master, but with their surplus time they could earn enough income to eventually buy their freedom.

By 1581–1583, the situation on the island could not have been worse. Spain sent the goods required by the population only after several years of delay, while prohibiting trade with non-Spanish colonies that were protected by an exclusive monopoly. This neglect, which continued into the nineteenth century, had a profound effect on the historical development of Santo Domingo and derailed the process of building the nation.

In the seventeenth century, an event of tremendous consequence, both for the future of the colony and for the slaves themselves, took place. By order of the Crown, Governor Osorio burned the entire west coast, forcing its depopulation, with the aim of preventing smuggling and dealing with pirates, buccaneers, and filibusters. Abandoned by the natives, the region was occupied, during the second half of the century, by a population of French origin. Under the protectorate of France, the settlement became the colony of Saint Domingue. In 1789, it consisted of 400,000 black slaves, 28,000 *manumisos*,[55] and 40,000 white Europeans.[56] In contrast, the Spanish part of the island had a total population of just 70,625 people, 8,900 of whom were slaves.

Demographic data is not always a valid reference for evaluating differences between two societies. In this case, the factual information is that two different economic models, simultaneous in space and time, produced two very different societies. While in the eighteenth century the plantation economy was thriving on the French side, the death of political and economic ties with the metropolis brought about a profound and paralyzing lethargy in the Spanish colony.

There was little to hope for within this desolate picture. However, Juan Bosch has observed a rebound by the middle of the century that was caused mainly by the production of ginger, sold cheaply in Spain. This positive period, however, did not continue long enough to produce significant change.[57]

Probably as a result of this momentary recovery, the demand for blacks to work in different areas of production increased. In response, on April 12, 1786, the Crown produced the "Real Cédula de Madrid" (Royal Charter of Madrid), giving the settlers the freedom to import an unlimited number of blacks, claiming no rights or responsibility for their fate provided they were engaged in fieldwork. Furthermore, agriculture, sugar-plantation goods, and apparel were exempted of all charges and taxes.

The royal charter also contained some provisions on the status of blacks, among which were:

- Assign a kind of annual tribute to blacks working in domestic service.
- Develop a moral, social, and economic code regulating their lives, the wording of which was assigned to a committee.
- Round up blacks who were vagabond or lazy to engage them in productive work.

These provisions reoriented the relations of sociocultural groups that for more than two centuries had inhabited the island under precarious conditions. The measures also represented a belated effort to define an economic project in the colony.

Despite these measures, the commencement of the Haitian Revolution in the late eighteenth century triggered reaction in the slaves on the Spanish side—reaction that was quickly stifled. The degree of identification among blacks of both colonies reached a climax with the short-lived occupation of the Spanish side by Toussaint Louverture in 1801 and his abolition of slavery, as had happened in Haiti. The slaves of Hispaniola had to wait to achieve their goal until 1822, when another Haitian occupation was installed that lasted twenty-two years. The movement also attracted the sympathies of *mulatos*, who, along with blacks, have historically been in the majority.[58]

Black Rebellions

Resistance of blacks to the living conditions of slave labor did not emerge for the first time in the Americas. From the moment of their capture, they refused to accept their new captive slave status. Although this form of economic subjugation was already known in Africa, the participation of companies dedicated to this new business increased the demand for, and subsequently the persecution of, blacks. Paradoxically, some African regimes—not just Europeans—made slavery a profitable business.

Capture was followed by temporary imprisonment in kingdoms that sanctioned slavery, and from there to the slave ships, to "change of place without change of color," as Fernando Ortiz put it.[59] During the voyage, punishment was continuous. When a slave was detected suffering from yellow fever, he was thrown into the sea with all of those who were on the same level or floor of the ship.

Suicide, the so-called "fixed melancholy" (loss of the will to live), and other forms of resistance were common during the voyage. Of the estimated

20 to 25 million slaves who crossed the Atlantic, some 5 million perished, which clearly shows the extent of the abuse to which they were subjected. According to Daniel Mannix and Malcolm Cowley: "These poor people were also crowded and largely shackled, making it difficult for them to turn around, stand, move or attempt to lie down without hurting themselves or others. More than once, a dead man and a living one were found stuck to one another."[60]

This fraught situation caused violent reactions in many cases. Between 1699 and 1845, around fifty-five mutinies occurred. On the coastlines of the Americas, blacks were sold after selection: first the sick, then the *"arrebañados"* (healthy, and sold in groups). In some cases, when these blacks became slaves, they were branded with a red-hot iron to identify them as belonging to a particular master.

Conditions such as these, compounded by overexploitation in sugarcane plantations and in gold mines, caused constant escapes. The motivating factor of this behavior was the uprooting from their natural environment and, equally important, from their psycho-emotional environment and culture.

To comprehensively understand their escape from plantations requires not only an understanding of the unbearable conditions of their existence, but also a consideration of their need to rebuild in a new land their own cultural references, social memory, in the so-called *cimarrón* cities.[61]

Hispaniola saw the emergence of several of these cities (also known as *manieles, cumbes, quilombos, palenques,* and *mocambos*), each with different characteristics.

- Some were simple temporary settlements of nomadic groups.
- Others, although more permanent, were formed by groups always ready to emigrate.

• The third and last type was known as a camp (*campamento*)[62]; in this case the guiding criterion was not the settlement, but a militarily defensible territorial and political organization, where the economy played a role in group continuity.

It is possible that these types of settlements were different from those that raided the cities under colonial power, plundering and harassing their inhabitants. For some scholars of the survival of African cultures in the Americas, these settlements were ways to try and reproduce, as truly as possible, ancestral cultural values, and to enjoy the only feasible way of liberty in a frankly hostile colonial society. These towns coexisted for over one hundred years with the colonial European society, becoming true community centers. Under these circumstances, they represent a powerful source for the study of the black presence in the Americas, although many have considered that the rebels assimilated European cultural patterns.

The history of the island of Santo Domingo not only records the first rebellion of blacks in the Americas, but it has also established a concrete expression of the class struggle between masters and slaves from the sixteenth to the nineteenth centuries. Of course, these forms of struggle also reflected the ups and downs of the economic model from which they originated.

In the overcrowded colony of Saint Domingue, Haitian struggles easily achieved a high level of tension due to the intensity of labor exploitation. Haiti was the model sugar-cane plantation economy, which inevitably led to the outcome known to all: the Haitian Revolution, as bloody as the relationships that served to support the French colonial model.

In Santo Domingo, black resistance began at the very dawn of slavery, in 1503, with the uprising of those who came to work in the gold mines. Although *ladinos*—as originally required by the colony because they knew the language, religion, and customs of their masters—the degree of mistreatment to which they were subjected was unbearable, especially because in Spain, blacks were linked to servitude, not to forced labor.

This first rebellion would change the minds of the governors on the island, who abandoned their original criteria about black *ladinos* and characterized them even more harshly as subversion and flights multiplied. Nevertheless, this situation did not preclude growth in the demand for slave labor and consequently its importation. As a precautionary lesson against new rebellions, blacks recaptured underwent terrible ordeals that sought to achieve two objectives: (1) show the other blacks what would be their fate if they rebelled, and (2) show the colony's neighbors the weight and presence of authority in order to avert suspicion and panic.

The continued economic decline caused the *Jerónimos* to apply for import licenses to boost the fledgling sugar industry. They preferred black *bozales* (i.e., blacks captured in Africa who did not know the language or culture of their masters) brought directly from Africa, considered more docile and obedient workers.

The first slave rebellion took place in 1552 at the plantation of Diego Colón, on the shores of the Isabela River, and it was led precisely by black *bozales.* Initiated by twenty slaves, most of them *jelofes wolof,* it united some forty conspirators, who killed several Spaniards. The rebellion spread to other plantations, but had a sad end for blacks. Many of them died in clashes with the whites; others were hanged or tortured.

There were numerous reasons for these rebellions, among them the hunger and punishments endured. According to C. E. Deive: "If a master (owner) wanted to punish a slave for some wrongdoing... instead of giving dinner... he would throw him to the floor, hands and feet tied, beating him with a piece of wood until his flesh would weep blood."[63]

Another reason, suggested by Manigat, was the lack of black women, because for a long time only black males were bought.[64] Many times, blacks would run away with the intention of finding a mate in the *manieles*.

The year 1540 recorded one of the most spectacular uprisings, led by Sebastián Lemba, considered one of the most important rebel leaders. Historians differ on the number of men under his command, giving figures ranging between 150 and 400 men.

His death, in September 1547, did not lead to the end of the rebellions; they lasted until the end of the eighteenth century. In 1796, about 200 slaves concentrated on the plantation of Juan Oyazal in Boca Nigua revolted against their masters, set the reeds on fire, and killed the cattle. As with others who had preceded them, the participants were defeated and tormented or hanged.

The influence of the "slaves' revolution" in Haiti was noticeable on the Santo Domingo side of the island. For a long time, the slaves on both sides shared the resistance to their conditions. Often the slaves of Saint Domingue were present or sought refuge in the conspiracies engendered in the west; or after the independence of Haiti, the slaves of Santo Domingo crossed the border in search of freedom. The Haitian revolutionary movement was cause for contagious enthusiasm, and even had the indirect support of their fellows, as was the case in the "conspiracy of Hinches" in the border area, now Haitian territory.

The first decades of the nineteenth century were also marked by sporadic signs of rebellion, which were suppressed—including that of Mendoza and Mojarra in 1812, cited by Roberto Cassá as reflecting the high degree of discontent in the colony, and especially showing how people of color began to consider union with Haiti as the most expeditious way to resolve their problems.[65]

The Mendoza and Mojarra episode marked the end of the era of black resistance to the condition of slavery. After the occupation of the Spanish side of the island by Haiti in 1822—viewed with sympathy by blacks and mulattos—another phase in black history began with the struggle for national independence in 1844, the restoration of the First Republic in 1863, and other important political events of the last 150 years. However, blacks would no longer view themselves as slaves, but as *creoles*, with feelings of patriotism, nationalism, and a new ethos that culturally defined them as Dominican citizens.

This sense of identity, however, did not arise with the struggles for independence. Its roots are to be found in the *cimarronaje*,[66] by which they resisted the Spanish ethnocide. It did not, however, reach critical levels to maintain and re-create a model culturally different from the rest of the society. For the black *cimarrón* on the Spanish side of the island, cohabitation with whites produced an inevitable syncretism. Certainly, they managed to keep some expression of African culture, but a good part of it had already been permeated by the colonial culture at the time of its flight.

Archbishop Portillo documented this shift after his visit in 1794 to the *cimarrón* community Los Naranjos: "Black *cimarrones* had memorized some prayers, and had been attending mass and, at least externally, seemed to be leading a Christian life."[67]

It is important, though, to bear in mind that in spite of the *cimarronaje*, both blacks and whites born in the Americas were forming a new culture based on the reinterpretation of everyday life and the need to build an adaptive new reality resulting from their experiences. In this slow process began a new self-image that would make them perceive themselves as *creole*—separate from the culture of their ancestors—and become Dominican citizens.

Ceremonial food left for the Baron of the cemetery. This offering corresponds in the Christian calendar to San Elias of Monte and Carmelo. The food consists of rice with black kidney beans and herring adorned with white candles as part of a service. It is served with pumpkin or higuero.

This altar of the deceased was constructed to honor June Rosemberg, a North American anthropologist, on the anniversary of her death.

A drum tribute offered upon the cabo de año *(anniversary of a death) of June Rosemberg.*

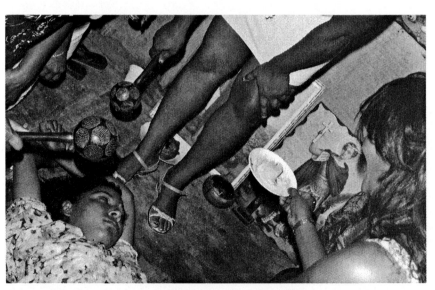

A possession in the presence of a Priestess of the Vudu and her companions in northern Santo Domingo.

Preparation of ceremonial food for a ceremony in memory of the deceased.

A Vudu Priestess in front of Saint Michel's Church, wearing Vudu Belie Belkan clothes.

A woman practicing the African tradition of carrying a load on the head.

Guloyas of San Pedro de Macorís dancing a traditional dance.

African drums are frequently used in Dominican religious ceremonies.

Ceremonial food offered to Vudu Deities.

Shanks at the Carnival of Santo Domingo.

A Dominican Vudu priestess performing a peanut ceremony.

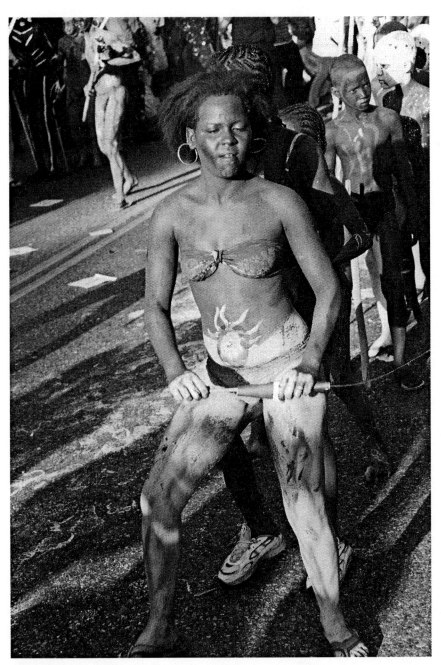

Pintaos dancers in Barahona.

Contributions of Black Culture
to Dominican Culture

I n a society with a significant presence of black cultural elements and an equally important ethnic composition of blacks and mulattos, one might think that it would be an easy and acceptable topic to approach.[68] However, it is not. Dominicans have suffered a slow and gradual process of alienation regarding their ethnocultural identity.

The result has been the ideological denial of African culture, and the distortion of the *homus cultural* that has placed Dominicans back in their historical past. In other words, back to their *real cultural being*, which has been replaced by a *fictitious cultural being*.

Once in the Americas, black Africans had to assume another form of expression—not only emotionally and psychologically, but also culturally. Their social memory constituted the reconstructive pillar of their needs in the new and hostile conditions. The black Africans reinterpreted and re-created things, eliminating what was inappropriate to the circumstances and to survival. Similarly, Africanness would pervade the new culture in an unavoidable symbiotic manner, despite the hidden traditional pro-Hispanic ideology. This is a noticeable phenomenon of all colonial societies in the Americas that involved slavery, and cannot be denied by nonsensical Manichaeism.

Thus, it will be the work of scholars (historians, anthropologists, linguists, archaeologists, musicologists, etc.) to determine the degree of ethnocultural involvement of the black component in the formation of these new societies, and specify which of the manifestations of everyday life are assumed, consciously or subconsciously, explicitly or implicitly. Five centuries of cohabitation cannot be ignored by the scientific discourse. African society—and its descendant: the mulatto or creole society—is an objective reality, whose existence is independent of our consciousness.

So far, the presence of African elements is generally admitted in at least two basic features of our culture: religion and music, and its creative and inspirational source. The African element is rhythm and mysticism; it is dance and ritual. Their world in a single principle integrates the sacred and the secular, the pain and the joy. The masks worn in sacred burial mock death and hide pain.

In the everyday life of the African world there is no contradiction between life and death, between music and religion, between the real world (secular) and the world of the ancestors (sacred). It is, in fact, an unaware mind that does not understand the notion of "capital sin." Such a society subjected to the humiliating process that slavery represented could not help but project its past onto the present and thus create its own psychic space. In the long run, the establishment of what could be called the "American identity" would blend with other cultural heritages, particularly the Spanish.

Each of our gestures, our food, colors, dances, music—as well as some religious expressions, turns of phrase, names of places, burial rites, crafts, and other objects—bear witness to that past.

Evidence of that is the presence/persistence of blackness in those things in which people routinely partake: food, gestures, form and color of dress, dance and music, religious beliefs, turns of phrase, place names, funeral rites, artisanship, and objects that represent culture in a material way.

MAGIC-RELIGIOUS MANIFESTATIONS

Magic-religious manifestations reflect the mixture of African-Christian elements, especially in populous urban and rural areas. The explanation for this fusion of beliefs lies in the colonial past, when blacks' religious practices and rites were prohibited.[69] These bans forced blacks to rethink their gods and beliefs. Cultural syncretism is enforced as a reaction to the denial of space and spiritual freedom, as expressed by Jorge Cela: "The American black acquires the gestures of his new culture but retains African thought. . . . He re-thinks Christianity through his own utilitarian and collective religion."[70]

It is within this exclusion process—governed by ethnocentric ideas—that Dominicans have forged an awareness of their cultural being. As in music, the magic-religious African roots will emerge, making the study of popular religion a point of paramount importance in the research of Dominican culture as a whole. Among the diverse set of practices, "Dominican voodoo"[71] is the greatest expression of African culture:

- The worshiping of deities (Papa Legba, Metre Silí, Papá Candelo, Anaisa, Pier Danton, Damballah, Baron of the Cemetery, etc.)
- Worship that is basically familial, without churches or altars; a practice within the home

- The offering of food and other ceremonial goods
- Drum-beating in honor of the deities, gods, mysteries, or *luases*[72]
- The spiritual possession of a *lua* or "mystery horse" (person who is "possessed" by deities)
- Relationships based on material interest, duties, rights, and punishment between the believer or practitioner and the deities
- Belief in ancestors, and ceremonies in their honor
- Celebrations to honor the deities (ceremonial food, animal sacrifice, musical rituals, dances, possession, etc.)

These manifestations are, in essence, of African origin. They are known primarily in rural and populous urban sectors. Repression or prejudices have never kept the population from a religious practice by which it is deeply influenced.

Other manifestations of popular religiosity have been equally affected by a syncretic process. Examples of this are the *cofradías* or "brotherhoods" (*cabildos*, "nations") known elsewhere in the Americas, although in the beginning the participation of blacks was forbidden for reasons of racial segregation.[73] Equally important are the practices associated with the cult of the dead.

The organization of the brotherhoods comes from the very beginning of the colony; one of them (1503) was the "Pure and Simple Conception of Our Lady." Two black-only fraternities, "St. John the Baptist" and "The Holy Spirit," were founded later. The basic objective of these organizations was to function as a society for religious burial and mutual aid. The first enabled the continuation of the cult of the dead and ancestors.

Linked to this system of religious beliefs is a rich and varied tradition: the cult of the dead. Its characteristic features correspond to the type of predominant ethnic settlement. For example, in the north of the country, with a low proportion of blacks, the prevalent practice is mainly Hispanic.

The Christian world perceives death as the end of a cycle that began at birth. As an unknown world, it is frightening. Death, its rites and ceremonies, become mandatory, but not vital to the survival of the group. Thus, after the tradition known as the "nine days," concluded with a mass, the relationship with the deceased will be only the memory of him. Contact with his world or spirit will be avoided. In rural areas where most of these beliefs prevail, death is associated with a set of perceptions not validated by Christian orthodoxy.

By contrast, in human groups where black presence is predominant, such as those in the central-south of the Dominican Republic who come from the Congo-Angola tradition, death carries a connotation similar to that of most African peoples.

African traits in the cult of the dead in these areas are:

- Drum-beating (*congo-atabales*) and dance
- Ceremonial celebration held throughout the day, involving—in addition to family—friends and neighbors in the community
- Food, alcoholic drinks, and confectionery
- The offering (of coffee, water, blessed candles) to the deceased because it is believed that his soul is present on "his holy day"; that is, there is no separation between the world of the living and the world of the dead
- Coexistence between the religious and the secular (folk tales of erotic content during the vigil, etc.)
- In many cases, "possession" of a member of the family by the spirit of the deceased or another spirit.

There are still other beliefs and practices that, although integrating Christian elements, are predominantly of black African origin.

Another ritual associated with death is the *baquini*, or burial of an "angel" (a child dead before committing sin). Although some researchers say this ritual is rooted in the Middle Ages, it is also recorded in Africa. There is probably a juxtaposition here, but not a contradiction of elements. It is also regarded as a possibility that these beliefs have made possible the partial cohesion of the black element in the Americas, to allow the reinterpretation of the inner world and societal reproduction.

Music

We find very strong African roots in music, especially that of religious origin. According to Martha Ellen Davis, Dominican music has a distribution of notes that reflects the influence of certain areas of Africa: the Congo, Cameroon, and Angola in the south-central part of the country, and Guinea in the north.[74] Naturally, the rhythms and musical genres are not expressed in a pure state. Also evident are the elements of Hispanic origin. The same happens with dance.

Among musical instruments, those made out of animal skins (*membranófonos*) retain more of an African imprint: the *atabales* (small drums) and some *salves* (chants) played with the *pandeiro* (tambourine). Fradique Lizardo believes the *canoita* (a kind of rattle) and the congo drums to be of African origin.[75] In these cases, as noted by Ellen Davis, "The scale is diatonic, i.e., modern European, but the pace is likely to have Congo-Angola influence. The structure is the African solo and chorus . . . but the chorus consists of a short sentence, or else a quartet."[76]

We also find improvisation, which is an African musical element. In the playing of *atabales*, this happens frequently, mainly with the *palo mayor* (large drum) serving the others as rhythmic bass. Considered sacred, the *atabales* are played in large parts of the country during festivals or religious ceremonies. Playing for fun is restricted.

The manufacture of the *atabales* is part of the folk tradition, and although its structure varies from one region to another, it follows a similar pattern— a tree trunk is hollowed out, and a patch of cow leather is fastened with either strong wooden pegs, metal rings, or rope. Those that are believed to have Guinean origins possess two goat-leather patches, as in the Congo-Angola tradition, in which music, dance, and liturgy are also distinctive.

Another instrument, no longer used, is the *arco de tierra* or *gayumba*, one of the few with no social use. The *marimba*, an instrument of music for fun, is a re-creation of the African *sanza*. In the case of the tambourine, used in the accompaniment of the *salve*, although of European origins, the addition of a rattle at the edges makes it a kind of African hand drum.[77]

The polyrhythm or mixture of sounds, primarily an African tradition, is frequently found in music with *membranófonos*, such as the *salve* and the *atabales*. Fradique Lizardo highlights the African influence in *sarandunga* dancing (music played in the church by black groups belonging to the confraternity of Saint John the Baptist in the south of the country), the *congos* and the *jaiba*.[78] However, the music of *atabales* (also commonly called *palos*, "sticks") is the one more clearly defined as having African roots.

OTHER ELEMENTS OF AFRICAN ORIGIN

Diet

Other areas of investigation are eating habits. In almost every society, these are evidence of the levels of social interaction between two or more people. The diet in a country, its food, ways of preparation, seasoning, cooking, restrictions, etc., allow a symbolic reading of its cultural past and the whole of its ethnic elements.

In Santo Domingo, in addition to conventional African-European food, there are also some foods of Taíno origin (*casabe*, for example) as well as some culinary techniques. Stews and condiments are an example of assimilation of African cooking methods, as well as consumption of specific agricultural products: bananas, green peas, yams (*ñame*).

According to C. E. Deive: "The use of the word *plátano* [banana] that appears in the chronicles of the Mártir de Anglería, Fernández de Oviedo, and Padre Acosta lasted throughout the sixteenth century. The word *guandul* [green peas] is linked to the word *kikongo, wandu* of Congolese origin. Some, like *mofongo*, retain their lexical origin."[79]

Other foods have gradually been incorporated into the Dominican diet as a result of inter-Caribbean and Haitian migration. Such is the case of the *chaco* and the *chenchen*, two dishes of the Haitian culinary tradition. Traditional Dominican cooking also includes dishes from the islands of St. Kitts and Tortola, from immigrants arriving in Santo Domingo in the nineteenth century to work in the sugar industry. From them remain the *calalún*, the *fungi*, and others.

Linguistics

African heritage is also expressed at the phonetic and morphological levels. In the manner in which Spanish is popularly spoken by Dominicans, the final *s* is often omitted, and the *r* is frequently changed to an *l*. Some word endings are cut. This is more common in areas of black settlement.

Toponymy

Toponymy has recorded a long list of names similar to places in Africa: Angola, Cambita, Congo, Fula, Lemba, Mandinga, Maniel, Palava, Calingá, Palenque, Naga, etc.

Group Work and Revolving Credit

Especially in rural areas, there is a form of group labor often called the *convite*, labor among neighbors for the purpose of preparing a field for planting or harvesting, or for building a house. People participate only in exchange for food and beverages. The beneficiary of the activity must commit to participate in similar activity organized by others.

Although this form of mutual aid is also known in the south of Spain, it is in Africa where it seems more widespread. According to Herskovits, the *dokpwe* of Dahomey is comparable to these forms of association and collective work in the Americas, and in particular in the Dominican Republic.[80]

Another example is the credit facility known as the *san*. It is similar to the Nigerian *ususu*, which has comparable characteristics. Benefits are awarded according to the place the person holds in a list. It is similar to the modern savings account.

Conclusions

The theme of the black presence in the Americas requires a lot more research to elucidate the process of transculturation and historical development between the fifteenth and the eighteenth centuries. Research should not only benefit the study of black communities. It is also necessary to explain, always with a critical eye, the quality of Indian and Spanish contributions. Only thus can we overcome cultural dichotomies and identify to what extent—in Santo Domingo in particular—the creation or redesign of adaptive modes of the original inhabitants, conquerors, settlers, and black slaves have merged to make way for a new culture.

The story should be demystified. By so doing, we acknowledge that despite the violence of the conquerors and colonizers, certain degrees of interaction were achieved, which made possible American societies as we know them today.

Denied by the colonial power, the "real cultural being" transfers its space to alienation. Dominican culture has taken shape according to someone else's categories, and above all, under someone else's judgments, prejudices, and feelings. Abandoning science, we have assumed the ideology of the colonizer.

In Santo Domingo and the rest of the Caribbean, social memory only works at a subconscious level, driven more by instinct than by reason. The opaqueness of the cultural memory ends up obscuring history itself. Otherwise the *hispanofília* of our official discourse would not have developed to such a degree at the expense of black history and its cultural components.

The Dominican Republic has the peculiarity of having gone through three different colonial economies: gold, the sugar industry in the sixteenth century, and cattle herding, which began at the end of the sixteenth century and continued far into the nineteenth century. This dislocation suffered at the early stages of the colonial economy would produce slavery relations *sui generis*.[81]

See what Tolentino Dipp has to say on this matter: "Before the development of the sugar industry, and even in its early days, there was not in America, as a central argument of the slavery ideology, racial prejudice against blacks. . . . It was later in time that the colonial oligarchy developed racial prejudices that served to justify the exploitation of black labor."[82]

This statement reveals the development process of an ideology that not only allowed the accumulation of vast fortunes at the expense of an overexploitation of black labor, but also built a hierarchy and defined the interaction between blacks and whites. This process outcome is what we see today in Dominican society.

Notes

1. Dictator who imposed his tyranny on Dominicans, 1930–1961.
2. Although we may find rather manipulated and "populist" ways of expression.
3. The "real cultural being" is the one that arises in the objective process of sociohistorical development, becoming the only possible way to look at the true identity of a people because it expresses its genesis, its ontogeny.
4. First Symposium: "African Presence in the West Indies," Universidad Autónoma de Santo Domingo, 1973.
5. Despite the resentment it may raise, this term is used in a nonpejorative way. It was originally used by colonialists to refer to the offspring of blacks and whites.
6. F. Lizardo refers to 70 percent mulattos, 10 percent blacks, and 16 percent whites. F. Lizardo, *Cultura africana en Santo Domingo* (Santo Domingo: Sociedad Industrial Dominicana, 1979).
7. The conscious mind expresses itself openly, especially against Haitians. The subconscious permeates even the language and the mood of the people, as well as other more subtle expressions.
8. Series of lectures on Black Folklore in Peru, Museo del Hombre Dominicano/ Ciasca, Santo Domingo, 1989.

9. One way of naming the cultural phenomenon. In the last century, Marcel Mauss and Emile Durkheim called the object of study in sociology the "social fact" or the "total social fact."

10. The emergence of religious syncretism in what are known as *luases* (gods, saints, and spirits of voodoo) and their link to Catholic saints had to do with the need of Africans to express their spiritual beliefs, which was forbidden by the masters. During the practice of their ceremonies, they would place the images of Catholic saints as substitutes for their gods. This type of behavior would also be displayed in other areas to meet their magic-religious needs, and would also become part of their cultural ways.

11. In R. Bastide, *Les religions afro-bresiliennes* (Paris: Copia mimeo, 1964).

12. UNESCO, "África entre los siglos xii–xvi," in *Historia general de África* (Paris: Editorial Tecnos, 1985).

13. Ibid.

14. Ibid.

15. *Malinkes*: from Mali.

16. UNESCO, "África entre los siglos xii–xvi."

17. Ibid.

18. Ibid.

19. F. L. Da Veiga Pinto, *La participacion de Portugal en la trata negrera del siglo xv al xix* (Paris: UNESCO, 1981).

20. Ibid.

21. F. Ortiz, *Los negros esclavos* (Havana: Ciencias Sociales, 1975).

22. According to Carlos Esteban Deive, there is a belief that perhaps some *ladino* slaves arrived in the second voyage of Christopher Columbus. Rolando Mallafe, cited by Deive, says about it: "We have reason to believe that some of the gentlemen who accompanied C. Columbus on his second trip brought their slaves with them." C. E. Deive, *La esclavitud del negro en Santo Domingo (1492 1844)* (Santo Domingo: Museo del Hombre Dominicano, 1981), 150.

23. J. Saco, *Historia de la esclavitud* (Madrid: Jucar, 1974).

24. Priests from the Order of Saint Jeronimo in Spain who became missionaries in Hispaniola.

25. Father Las Casas and Fernando Oviedo refer to sugar production in the city of La Vega for consumption on the island only, because there was not enough for export.

26. J. García, *África en Venezuela: Pieza de Indias* (Caracas: Cuadernos Lagoven, 1980).

27. *Moros*: a name given by the Spanish to the unbaptized.

28. F. Moya Pons, *La Española en el siglo xvi (1453 1520)* (Santiago, Dominican Republic: Universidad Católica Madre y Maestra, 1973).

29. Ortiz, *Los negros esclavos*.

30. In D. Mannix and M. Cowley, *Historia de la trata de negros* (Madrid: Alianza Editorial, 1970).

31. Rafael Lopez Valdez, in his lecture "Africanía in Cuba," delivered at the Museo del Hombre Dominicano in 1991, referred to an informant descended from slaves in Cuba as coming from a part of Africa "where the sun was dying behind him," i.e., the east coast.

32. Mannix and Cowley, *Historia de la trata de negros*.

33. Cited by García in *África en Venezuela*.

34. Ortiz, *Los negros esclavos*.

35. Ibid.

36. C. Larrazábal Blanco, *Los negros y la esclavitud en Santo Domingo* (Santo Domingo: J. D. Postigo, 1975), 86–87.

37. Ibid., 57.

38. Ortiz, *Los negros esclavos*.

39. C. E. Deive, "Topónimos dominicanos vinculados a esclavos y a África," *Boletín del Museo del Hombre Dominicano*, no. 14 (1980).

40. Ibid.

41. *Ethnonym*: from *ethno* and *name*.

42. Lizardo, *Cultura africana en Santo Domingo*; Larrazábal Blanco, *Los negros y la esclavitud en Santo Domingo*.

43. O. B. Yai, *Ethnonymie et toponymie africaines: réflexions pour une décolonisation* (Paris: UNESCO, 1984), 43.

44. H. Tolentino Dipp, *Raza e historia en Santo Domingo* (Santo Domingo: Universidad Autónoma d Santo Domingo, 1974).

45. Moya Pons, *La Española en el siglo xvi (1453–1520)*.

46. Juan Bosch was president of the Dominican Republic in 1963. See J. Bosch, *Composición social dominicana* (Santo Domingo: Amigo del Hogar, 1976).

47. Cited by Saco in *Historia de la esclavitud*.

48. *Ladino*: a slave who had already been in contact with European civilization and therefore knew the language, customs, etc., as opposed to *bozal*: a slave who came directly from Africa.

49. Tolentino Dipp, *Raza e historia en Santo Domingo*.

50. J. Bosch and H. Tolentino Dipp address the problem of the island's population by not only analyzing the information available, but calculating according to the process of depopulation that was occurring at that time, and the economic unit that the plantation represented. In 1550 there were around thirty mills, with an average population of 150 black slaves, resulting in about 4,500 people. J. Bosch, *Composición social dominicana*; H. Tolentino Dipp, *Raza e historia en Santo Domingo*, 164–65.

51. *Almojarifazgo*: a tax charged for the merchandise that was traded to, from, or within the Spanish kingdom territories.

52. Larrazábal Blanco, *Los negros y la esclavitud en Santo Domingo*, 37.

53. Saco, *Historia de la esclavitud*.

54. José Antonio Saco, *Historia de la esclavitud* (Madrid: Júcar, 1974), 181.

55. *Manumisos*: slaves who have bought their freedom.

56. R. Silié, *Economía, esclavitud y población* (Santo Domingo: Universidad Autónoma de Santo Domingo, 1976).

57. Bosch, *Composición social dominicana*.

58. See F. Moya Pons "La primera abolicion de la esclavitud en Santo Domingo," *EME-EME* 3, no. 19 (July–August 1974): 13.

59. Ortiz, *Los negros esclavos*.

60. Mannix and Cowley, *Historia de la trata de negros*. Translation is from the Spanish edition.

61. *Cimarrón* is a creole word originally associated with animals in the wild, and rebellions of the Indians. Later it was used to name the uprisings of blacks in the Americas. It was first used in the Spanish colony of Santo Domingo in the uprisings led by the chief Enriquillo in the south, in the second decade of the sixteenth century. Well-known cities founded by the rebels are also called *cimarrónes*.

62. Deive, *Topónimos dominicanos vinculados a esclavos y a África*.

63. Ibid.

64. Ibid.

65. R. Cassá, *Historia social dominicana*, vol. 1 (Santo Domingo: Punto y Aparte, 1983);

Deive, *La esclavitud del negro en Santo Domingo*, 478.

66. *Cimarronaje*: first rebellions of Indians and blacks in the Americas.

67. C. E. Deive, *Los cimarrónes del maniel de Neiba: Historia y etnografía* (Santo Domingo: Banco Central de la República Dominicana, 1985).

68. Roger Bastide and other authors refer to the process of re-creation of cultural models that allowed blacks to survive the shameful level of exploitation—using only their social memory—and the creation of new cultural forms resulting from original patterns but in different historical circumstances. Hence it is called black culture rather than African culture.

69. All ordinances and provisions are found in the Código Negro Carolino of 1784 (Black Code).

70. J. Cela, "Sincretismo afro-americano: Introducción a un estudio comparado." *Revista de Estudios Sociales* Año 3 (Santo Domingo: Revista de Estudios Sociales, 1973).

71. There is no agreement among Dominican researchers about the name. While some believe these religious practices should not have a Haitian name because it generates confusion, others argue that, coming originally from Haiti, the description is correct. A third group argues for more comprehensive studies on the subject, in order to highlight Dominican particularities and maybe find a term less confrontational and at the same time more representative.

72. *Luases*: Haitian creole term that refers to the deities.

73. E. Rodriguez Demorizi defines as fraternities or sororities congregations of devout people gathered to exercise works of piety and Christian devotion (*Sociedades, cofradías, escuelas, gremios y otras corporaciones dominicanas* [Santo Domingo: Academia Dominicana de la Historia, 1975]).

74. M. E. Davis, *Las voces del purgatorio: Estudio de la salve dominicana* (Santo Domingo: Museo del Hombre Dominicano, 1981).

75. F. Lizardo, *Cultura africana en Santo Domingo* (Santo Domingo: Sociedad Industrial Dominicana, 1979).

76. Davis, *Las voces del purgatorio*.

77. Ibid.

78. F. Lizardo, *Cultura africana en Santo Domingo* (Santo Domingo: Sociedad Industrial Dominicana, 1979).

79. C. E. Deive, "Herencia africana en la cultura dominicana," in *Ensayos sobre cultura dominicana* (Santo Domingo: Museo del Hombre Dominicano, 1981).

80. In Deive, "Herencia africana en la cultura dominicana."

81. Silié, *Economía, esclavitud y población*; Bosch, *Composición social dominicana.*

82. Tolentino Dipp, *Raza e historia en Santo Domingo.*

Bibliography

Bastide, R. *Les Amériques noires*. Paris: Petite Bibliothèque Payot, 1967.

———. *Les religions afro-brésiliennes*. Paris: Copia mimeo, 1964.

Berteaux, P. *África desde la pre-historia hasta los Estados actuales.* 3rd ed. Madrid: Siglo XXI, 1974.

Bosch, J. *Composición social dominicana*. Santo Domingo: Amigo del Hogar, 1976.

Cassá, R. *Historia social dominicana*. Vol. 1. Santo Domingo: Punto y Aparte, 1983.

Cela, J. "Sincretismo afro-americano: Introducción a un estudio comparado." *Revista de Estudios Sociales* 3 (Santo Domingo: Revista de Estudios Sociales, 1973).

Cornevin, R., and M. Cornevin. *Histoire de l'Afrique*. 4th ed. Paris: Petite Bibliothèque Payot, 1964.

Da Veiga Pinto, F. L. *La participacion de Portugal en la trata negrera del siglo xv al xix*. Paris: UNESCO, 1981.

Davis, M. E. *La otra ciencia: El vudú como religión y como medicina popular*. Santo Domingo: Universidad Autónoma de Santo Domingo, 1987.

———. *Las voces del purgatorio: Estudio de la salve dominicana*. Santo Domingo: Museo del Hombre Dominicano, 1981.

Dean, E. *Historia en blanco y negro: Análisis de los manuales escolares en Sudáfrica*. Paris:

UNESCO, 1984.

Deive, C. E. *Los cimarrones del maniel de Neiba: Historia y etnografía.* Santo Domingo: Banco Central de la República Dominicana, 1985.

———. *La esclavitud del negro en Santo Domingo (1492 1844).* Santo Domingo: Museo del Hombre Dominicano, 1981.

———. "Herencia africana en la cultura dominicana." In *Ensayos sobre cultura dominicana,* ed. Virginia R. Domínguez and Bernardo Vega. Santo Domingo: Museo del Hombre Dominicano, 1981.

———. "Topónimos dominicanos vinculados a esclavos y a África." *Boletín del Museo del Hombre Dominicano,* no. 14 (1980).

———. *Vudú y magia en Santo Domingo.* Santo Domingo: Museo del Hombre Dominicano, 1979.

Fage, F., and R. Oliver. *Breve historia de África.* Madrid: Alianza Editorial, 1972.

Fanon, F. *Peau noire, masques blancs.* Paris: Seuil, 1952.

García, J. *África en Venezuela: Pieza de Indias.* Caracas: Cuadernos Lagoven, 1980.

Larrazábal Blanco, C. *Los negros y la esclavitud en Santo Domingo.* Santo Domingo: J. D. Postigo, 1975.

Lizardo, F. *Cultura africana en Santo Domingo.* Santo Domingo: Sociedad Industrial Dominicana, 1979.

———. *Instrumentos musicales folklóricos dominicanos.* Santo Domingo: UNESCO, 1988.

Malagón Barceló, J. *Código Negro Carolino (1784).* Santo Domingo: Ediciones Taller, 1974.

Mannix, D., and M. Cowley. *Historia de la trata de negros.* Madrid: Alianza Editorial, 1970. [*Black Cargoes: A History of the Atlantic Slave Trade* (New York: Viking Press, 1962)].

Métreaux, A. *Le vaudou haïtien.* Paris: Gallimard, 1958.

Moya Pons, F. *La Española en el siglo XVI (1453–1520).* Santiago, Dominican Republic: Universidad Católica Madre y Maestra, 1973.

———. "La primera abolicion de la esclavitud en Santo Domingo." *EME-EME* 3, no. 19 (July–August 1974).

———. *La primera abolición de la esclavitud en Santo Domingo.* Santiago, Dominican Republic: Universidad Católica Madre y Maestra, 1974.

Ortiz, F. *Los negros esclavos.* Havana: Ciencias Sociales, 1975.

Rodríguez Demorizi, E. *Sociedades, cofradías, escuelas, gremios y otras corporaciones dominicanas.* Santo Domingo: Academia Dominicana de la Historia, 1975.

Saco, J. *Historia de la esclavitud*. Madrid: Jucar, 1974.

Silié, R. *Economía, esclavitud y población*. Santo Domingo: Universidad Autónoma de Santo Domingo, 1976.

Tolentino Dipp, H. *Raza e historia en Santo Domingo*. Santo Domingo: Universidad Autónoma de Santo Domingo, 1974.

Tujibikile, M. *La resistencia cultural del negro en América Latina: Lógica ancestral y celebración de la vida*. Santo Domingo: Editorial DEI, 1990.

UNESCO. "África entre los siglos xii–xvi." In *Historia general de África*. Paris: Editorial Tecnos, 1985.

———. *La trata negrera del siglo xv al xix*. Paris: UNESCO, 1978.

Wolf, E., and Mintz, S. "Plantaciones." In *Haciendas, latifundios y plantaciones en América Latina*. México: Siglo Veintiuno Editores, 1975.

Yai, O. B. *Ethnonymie et toponymie africaines: réflexions pour une décolonisation*. Paris, UNESCO, 1984.